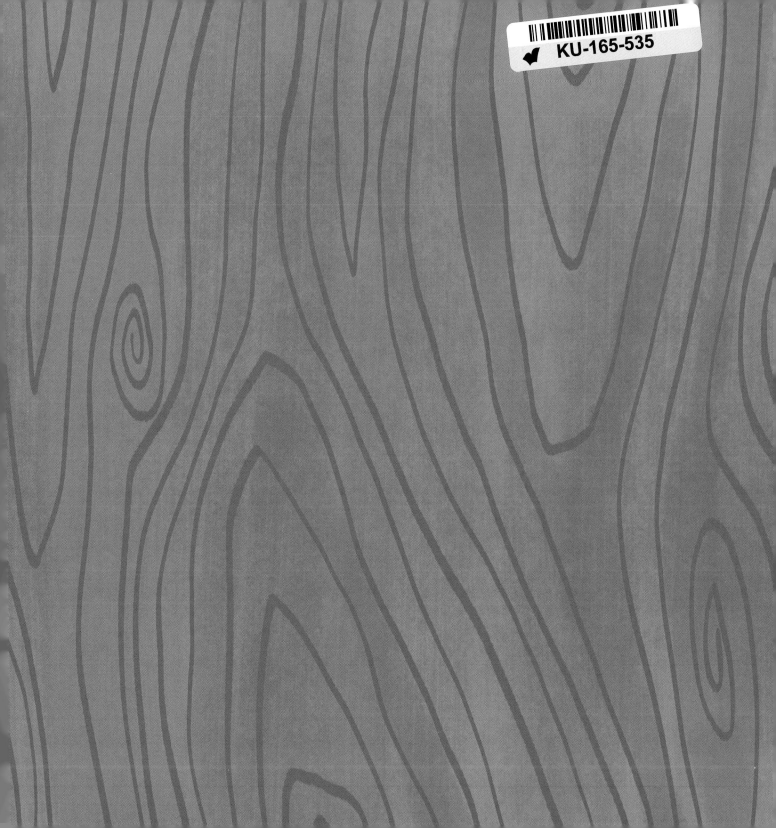

WRITTEN BY
Scott James

ILLUSTRATED BY
Geraldine Rodríguez

For my Benjamin,
To keep you company as you
watch for His return.

S.J.

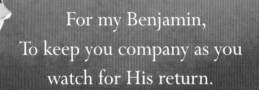

The Littlest Watchman
© Scott James / The Good Book Company 2017. Reprinted 2021.

"The Good Book For Children" is an imprint of The Good Book Company Ltd.
Email: info@thegoodbook.com

North America: www.thegoodbook.com UK: www.thegoodbook.co.uk
Australia: www.thegoodbook.com.au New Zealand: www.thegoodbook.co.nz

Illustrated by Geraldine Rodríguez / Art Direction & Design by André Parker
ISBN: 9781784981402 | Printed in India

*"My eyes are awake before the watches of the night,
that I may meditate on your promise."*

PSALM 119 v 148

Have you ever had to wait for a special gift? Maybe right now there's a beautifully wrapped present sitting under your Christmas tree, almost calling out to you with the promise of something wonderful inside.

Long ago, God's people found themselves waiting for something wonderful as well. They were waiting for a promise to come true. They were waiting, and watching…

One night on a quiet hillside, a little boy sat beside an old tree stump, watching and waiting.

His name was Benjamin, and he was a Watchman.

Being a Watchman was a pretty big job. Benjamin did his best to take it seriously. But the problem was that his main duty was to sit still and stare at a boring old tree stump, which made it kind of hard to stay interested.

Even so, he knew that the people in his village counted on him. Benjamin's father was also a Watchman and taught him all about it.

"You want me to stare at a tree stump?" Benjamin had asked when he first learned of the Watch.

"It's not about staring, son. It's about *waiting*," his father answered. "Every day and every night, one of us is watching. We watch for the sign of the arrival of the King, just like our Maker promised."

Benjamin's father had raised him to know the old, old stories of their people. He told him how once, long ago, their Maker created the world and everything in it. All of it was very good. And the Maker had created people to love him and care for his world.

But something went terribly wrong. The people chose to follow their own plans. They disobeyed their Maker, and in doing so allowed a curse to enter the land—the curse of sin.

The curse brought pain and sorrow into their lives and the lives of all their children. The world was still beautiful, but now, because of the curse, it was broken. Worst of all, the curse separated people from their Maker. Instead of living with him forever, they died.

It all seemed rather hopeless.

But things aren't always as they seem...

Benjamin's father taught him that their Maker had promised to send someone to undo the curse.

He promised to send them a King who would rescue them and restore the whole world. Instead of leaving them like a useless stump, the Maker promised that a new branch—one man—would grow his people into a fruitful tree. This man would come from the family of a man named Jesse.

The Maker told people to wait for his King and to trust in his promise.

The Watchmen *did* trust, and they did their best to help others trust. They reminded the people about what the Maker had said hundreds of years before:

> *"There shall come forth a shoot from the stump of Jesse, and a branch from his roots shall bear fruit."*

Even though the Maker had been awfully quiet for many years now, the Watchmen still trusted his promises and kept a close lookout for the arrival of the promised King.

Benjamin wanted to be a good Watchman, but he found it difficult.

For one thing, it had become really boring. He tried to focus by tracing the rings of wood on the stump, circling his eyes round and round as he thought about the Maker's promise. But as hard as he tried, it took only a skittering bug or the hoot of an owl to make him completely lose track of where he was.

Besides that, Benjamin struggled because everyone laughed at him. Sometimes, other children from the village would throw things at him as he tried to stare at the stump. It was all very distracting.

Then there were the shepherds. They often walked past him on their way to the fields. Most nights, Benjamin could hear them laughing and having a good time as they roamed the neighboring hillside.

"They have all the fun," Benjamin often thought. "They're not stuck looking at an old stump. I wish I could have been a shepherd instead of a Watchman."

Night after night Benjamin kept watch, hoping that the long-awaited shoot would appear on the stump. But it never did.

Nothing ever happened.

One day, it became even harder for Benjamin to focus.

The road below became very busy. Travelers started pouring past on the way to the village. There were people of all sorts—men and women, old and young, some on carts with donkeys, others walking. Benjamin even noticed a man helping a very pregnant woman slowly make her way along the road.

Along with all these distractions, something deeper started to trouble Benjamin. He had always believed the Maker would send the promised King, but he couldn't help but wonder what was taking so long. "Maybe we got the plan wrong," he began to think. "Maybe he's not coming at all." The thought left him confused, and a little ashamed.

Benjamin had waited a long time, and he wasn't sure if he could do it anymore.

He took his eyes off the stump.

Shoulders slumping, Benjamin looked toward the shepherds' hill. "Maybe I should just go become a shepherd," he thought. "It seems I'm not cut out to be a Watchman after all."

But as he gazed toward the shepherds, Benjamin's eyes squinted and then widened.

The shepherds were not alone.

In the sky above them, a single light shone down.

Suddenly, a glorious brightness lit up the night sky over the shepherds.

Shading his eyes, Benjamin could see a host of dotted lights within the larger glow. He couldn't make out the words but he could hear that the lights were singing. Joyously singing.

Benjamin sat spellbound as he took in the light and melody. It was so beautiful he never wanted it to end. And yet something drew his attention back to the old stump.

Benjamin's eyes had been trained to know every detail of the stump. It never changed. It had always been the same.

It wasn't now.

Growing out of the hardened wood on the top of the stump was a small... green... *shoot*.

A great flood of joy filled Benjamin as he remembered the Maker's promise.

"There shall come forth a shoot from the stump of Jesse, and a branch from his roots shall bear fruit."

Quick as he could, Benjamin jumped up and ran toward the village, down into Bethlehem, barely able to contain his excitement as he darted along the dark path.

As he reached the edge of the sleeping houses, the words burst out of his mouth in a great shout—

"He's here! He's here! The King has come!"

Just then, the door of a small building swung open and light from inside spilled out into the street.

And Benjamin heard a familiar voice—the voice of one of the shepherds:

"Yes, the King *has* come.

"Would you like to come in and meet him?"

You Can Join the Watch

The Bible may not mention anything about a little Watchman named Benjamin staring at a tree stump, but the imagery and the promises in this made-up story are all over God's word. The Old Testament is filled with promises about the coming Messiah—the King who would come to rescue his people from the curse of sin.

God, our Maker, promised, "There shall come forth a shoot from the stump of Jesse, and a branch from his roots shall bear fruit" (Isaiah 11 v 1). People who trusted God spent their lives waiting and watching for him to keep that promise. Sure enough, 700 years after the prophet Isaiah spoke God's promise, Jesus came—a baby from Jesse's family, the shoot sprouting from the stump, the King whom God had promised.

The Watchmen in this story were not real, but the events Benjamin saw on the shepherds' hill were. We call it Christmas.

At Christmas, we remember that Jesus was born so that he could live, die, and rise again to keep God's promise to rescue us. We remember that he ascended back into heaven and sat on his throne as the King he is.

But before Jesus went, he said, "I will come again and will take you to myself, that where I am you may be also" (John 14 v 3). King Jesus has promised that he is coming back for us! People who trust God today spend their lives waiting and watching for him to keep his promise.

We wait and watch by remembering what Benjamin learned: God always keeps his promises. One day, this world will see Jesus returning. Let's trust God so deeply that we look for him with excitement every single day.